HABITATS
Mountains

Robert Snedden

FRANKLIN WATTS
LONDON•SYDNEY

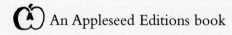 An Appleseed Editions book

First published in 2004 by Franklin Watts
96 Leonard Street, London, EC2A 4XD

Franklin Watts Australia
56 O'Riordan Street, Alexandria, NSW 2015

© 2004 Appleseed Editions

Created by Appleseed Editions Ltd,
Well House, Friars Hill, Guestling, East Sussex, TN35 4ET

Designed by Helen James

ISBN 0 7496 5714 6

A CIP catalogue for this book is available from the British Library.

Photographs by Corbis (Tiziana and Gianni Baldizzone, Tom Brakefield, W. Perry Conway, William Dow, John W. Herbst, Jeremy Horner, Steve Kaufman, W. Wayne Lockwood, M.D., Joe McDonald, David Muench, Francesc Muntada, NASA/Roger Ressmeyer, José F. Poblete, Annie Poole; Papilio, Galen Rowell, Kevin Schafer, Grafton Marshall Smith, Richard Hamilton Smith, Dale C. Spartas, Craig Tuttle, Jeff Vanuga, Bob Winsett, Michael S. Yamashita)

Printed and bound in Thailand

Contents

The world's high places

The place where a living thing makes its home is called its **habitat**. A habitat can be as small as a damp place under a rotting log, or as big as the ocean. The biggest habitats, such as deserts, forests and mountains, are called **biomes**.

Mountain climbing

There are mountains on all the world's continents. They cover about one-fifth of the Earth's land surface. Mountain habitats are rich and varied. Climbing a mountain can be like making a journey through the world's northern **climate** zones. If you climb a few hundred metres up a mountain, you can pass through a number of different biomes, from broad-leaved forest at the bottom of the mountain, to evergreen forest, grassland, **tundra** and the **alpine** biome just beneath the snowline.

About one-fifth of Earth's land surface is covered in challenging mountain habitat.

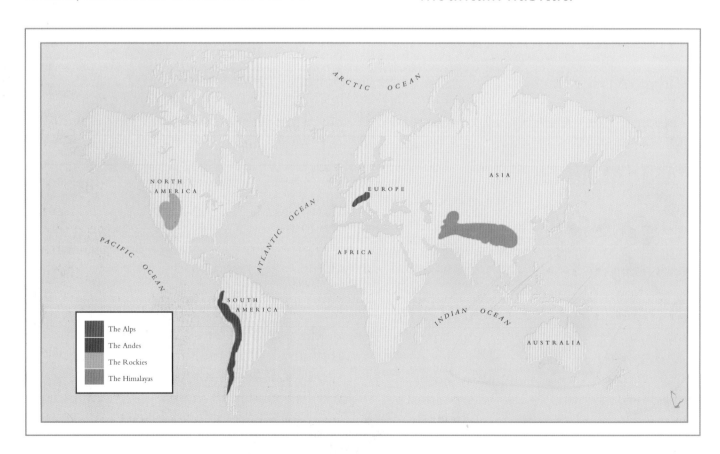

The Alps
The Andes
The Rockies
The Himalayas

Mountains look spectacular, but only the hardiest living things can survive at high altitudes.

Islands of life

Mountains have been described as islands of biodiversity, as many types of plants and animals survive there that have been crowded out of the lowland areas. The rapidly-changing conditions on a mountain challenge the survival of the plants and animals that live there. These include changes in **altitude**, the steepness of the slopes, exposure to the sun and the rise and fall of the temperature, high winds, rain and snow. Mountains are homes to living things that are found nowhere else in the world.

At the foot of a mountain, the wildlife is much the same as in the landscape around the mountain. Higher up is where the true mountaineers live – sure-footed animals and hardy plants that have adapted to life in the cold, rocky landscape of the high mountains.

The habitat changes you find as you climb higher up a mountain aren't exactly the same as those you would find if you journeyed northwards. As you travel north, the days become shorter during the winter. As you climb a mountain, the length of the days remains the same at the top as it is at the bottom. The tundra on a mountain is different from the tundra in the far north, too. At the top of the mountain, it is like winter all the time, although the days are longer for at least some of the year.

Mountain weather

A mountain's weather follows the same seasons and has the same wet and dry periods as the lowlands around it. Mountain climates can be represented by narrow bands stacked on top of each other. The temperature falls as the altitude increases. For every 100 metres of altitude, the temperature becomes cooler by about one degree.

So even if a mountain range happens to be in the middle of the tropics, it is still chilly high up. Tropical mountain climates can be rather odd. Frosts are frequent at high altitudes, even in summer. High up on a mountain the sun shines very brightly when the sky is clear. Because the air is thinner high up, the rays of the tropical sun can warm the ground very quickly.

However, thin air is no good at trapping heat, so as soon as the sun disappears, the temperature plummets again.

The higher the altitude, the lower the temperature. Mountain tops are cold places!

Mountains are often wet, too. Rising warm air carries moisture from below. As it rises, it cools, and the moisture forms clouds that wreathe the mountains. The tiny water droplets that form the clouds can be trapped by mountain plant life before they fall as rain.

Mountains are also much windier places than the surrounding lowlands. Since they are the highest things around, there is nothing to act as a windbreak to shield the mountains from the wind's full force.

Climate regulators

Mountains have a big effect on the weather patterns of the lower-lying areas around them. The grassy plains, or steppes, of northern Asia are kept dry by mountain ranges to the west and south. These ranges

The cool air around a mountain top, mixed with the warm, moist air rising from below, causes clouds to form.

block moist air moving in from the ocean and stop it from reaching the grasslands. In the winter, the mountains trap cold air flowing down from the Arctic, resulting in very cold winters. The Atacama Desert, in South America, is so effectively blocked by the Andes Mountains that it sometimes has no rain for several years at a time.

Mountains can also act as water storage depots. Water that has accumulated on the mountain tops in the form of snow and ice is released slowly into streams as the spring thaws come. These streams feed into rivers that provide water for the countryside below.

Mountain plants

The types of plants that grow on a mountainside are generally similar to the plants that grow on the lower-lying lands to the north of the mountain. This means, for example, that plants found high in the mountains of Great Britain are also found at lower levels in Norway.

Vegetation zones

Mountain plant life is divided into different regions of **vegetation**. At the bottom of the mountain are forests, above the forests are meadows, and above the meadows small plants grow among the rocks. These zones are a result of the changing conditions at different heights on the mountain.

There are warm summers and cool winters at the bottom of a mountain, in the **temperate zone**, just as there are in the surrounding landscape. These conditions suit broad-leaved trees that shed their leaves in the winter, such as oaks and maple trees. The lower slopes of the mountain are likely to be thickly forested.

Further up the mountain, conditions are cooler, just as they are in the northern forests. Broad-leaved trees cannot survive there. **Conifers**, or evergreen trees, are better suited to low temperatures. Conifers keep their dark-green leaves throughout the year. Dark leaves absorb heat from the sun more quickly than light-coloured leaves, and warm leaves make food faster than cold ones. By keeping their leaves all the year round, conifers are ready to make food whenever the sun appears. Their cone shape is another **adaptation**

Conifers, with their narrow evergreen leaves and conical shape, are well suited to life on the cool mountainside.

Above the tree line, hardy alpine flowers put on a colourful springtime show.

to high mountain life. Higher up there is more likelihood of snow, but it slips easily off the conifers without damaging their branches. Conifers also have shallow root systems that spread out widely in the thin soil on the mountainside.

The tree line

Above a certain height, conditions become so harsh that no tree can grow. This height is called the tree line. Below it lie the conifers, and above it lie no trees at all.

Although no trees grow above the tree line, smaller plants do. This area is called the alpine meadow, and in the spring, it can be covered in a dazzling display of flowers. There are few insects to act as **pollinators** there, so plants are brightly coloured to attract them. Higher up the mountain, the soil cover becomes even thinner, and the bare rock of the mountain top is exposed. Sometimes there are little pockets of soil trapped between rocks where hardy plants can take root. These high-altitude plants often have hairy leaves that trap what little warmth there is. Leaves are also dark coloured to absorb as much heat as possible from the sun. Alpine plants are much smaller than plants at lower altitudes. Tall plants would be torn apart by the winds.

MOUNTAIN TEAM

The only plants that grow on bare mountain rocks are lichens. A lichen isn't a flowering plant. It is a partnership between simple plants called algae and a fungus. The fungus grips the rock surface and produces chemicals that dissolve it, releasing **nutrients** for the algae. The algae make food from sunlight for both to share. It takes teamwork to survive in high mountains.

Mountain animals

Conditions at high altitudes present animals with a number of challenges to survival. High mountain conditions are similar to those in the polar regions, but there are important differences.

Keeping warm

An obvious challenge is keeping warm. Only warm-blooded animals can survive in the high mountain regions. No **reptiles** or **amphibians** can live there. Alpine animals have adapted to the cold in a number of ways. Some escape the worst of the winter cold by going into **hibernation** in a warm, secure den until conditions improve in the spring. Others **migrate** downwards to the warmer lower slopes of the mountains. Most mountain animals are protected from the cold by thick, furry coats and layers of insulating fat. The body shape of a mountain animal may be different from that of its lowland relatives. Its legs, tail, and ears are likely to be shorter. These adaptations reduce the loss of body heat.

Radiation proofing

Another high-altitude hazard comes from ultraviolet (UV) **radiation** from the sun. At lower levels, much of this harmful radiation

A sure-footed mountain goat moves confidently in its rocky home.

The vicuña's coat traps heat, insulating the animal from the cold mountain air.

is blocked out by the **atmosphere**, though it can still cause sunburn on unprotected skin in the summer. Mountain animals are often darkly coloured, as black pigment absorbs the harmful UV rays and helps prevent them from reaching the animal's sensitive internal organs where they could do serious damage. The downside is that dark colours are poor **camouflage** against the snowy backdrop of the high mountains.

Take a deep breath

As mountaineers and skiers who compete at high altitudes know, the air becomes thinner higher up, which means that oxygen isn't as plentiful. It can be difficult to breathe easily. Animals of the high mountains are adapted to this. They have larger lungs than low-altitude animals, and their blood carries more of the red blood cells that take oxygen from the lungs to the rest of the body. Mountain animals can have more than three times as many red blood cells as animals at lower levels.

People who live at high altitudes, such as the Sherpas of the Himalaya Mountains in Nepal, also have these 'high-life' adaptations. Animals that move up and down the slopes during the year make more red blood cells as they move back up to higher altitudes. Human mountain climbers can also become used to high altitudes in this way.

11

The Himalayas

The Himalayan mountain range curves across 2,400 kilometres of south-central Asia, crossing the countries of Bhutan, Nepal, Tibet, India and Pakistan. Many of these mountains reach higher than 5 kilometres above the plains around them. The name Himalaya means house of snow. The highest mountain in the world, Mount Everest, is there. Its peak is more than 8,845 metres above sea level.

Mountain seasons

The Himalayas are around the same distance from the **equator** as Florida, but because of the high-altitude conditions there, their climates are very different. High up, the air is very thin and dry – little rain (in the form of snow) falls there. It is very cold. Summers are short and cool, while winters are long and very cold, making the climate more like that of Alaska than

Pictures from space reveal the rugged landscape of the Himalayas.

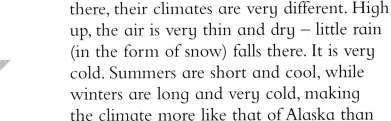

▲ *The rhododendron bush is a common plant of the Himalayan slopes.*

Florida. The average winter temperature is just above freezing, with January being the coldest month. The warmest month is June, with average summer temperatures of around 13° Celsius.

Further down the slopes, where the air is warm and moist, there are likely to be sudden downpours of rain in the summer and snowstorms in the winter. High winds can rip through the mountains at any time.

Himalayan mountain plants

Up to about 2,100 metres above sea level, chestnut trees, laurels and oaks grow on the lower mountains. Higher than this, broad-leaved trees give way to pine trees and other conifers. Rhododendron bushes and tea plants are common on most of the mountain slopes of the Himalayas.

These shrubs grow fairly close to the ground, allowing them to withstand high winds and freezing conditions. Above 3,700 metres, only grasses, mosses and lichens are tough enough to withstand the bitterly cold conditions.

Himalayan wildlife

On the lower slopes of the mountains at the southern end of the range, the mountain habitat blends into a tropical forest habitat. There, tigers, monkeys and Asian elephants live among the tropical plants. Higher up in the mountains are animals such as mountain goats, with their thick, warm coats and strong hoofs. One of the most common animals of the Himalayas is the yak, a long-haired member of the cattle family. Read about this remarkable animal on page 26.

The Andes

The Andes Mountains are one of the longest and highest of the world's great mountain ranges. They run for about 7,200 kilometres right along the western edge of South America, from Panama in the north to Cape Horn at the tip of Chile in the south. Many Andean peaks are more than 6,000 metres high. Only the Himalayas have higher peaks.

Andean climates

Because the Andes stretch for such a long way from north to south, there are great variations in climate. For this reason, the Andes are separated into three regions: the southern, central and northern Andes. The northern Andes lie close to the equator, so this is the hottest part of the range. The climate is hot and humid, and rainforests grow up the flanks of the mountains. The southern Andes are 6,400 kilometres to the south and approach the cold Southern Ocean and the **Antarctic Circle**. They are much colder, whereas the central Andes, positioned between the equatorial north and the near-Antarctic south, enjoy a milder climate.

The wide paramo grasslands stretch out across the high plains of the Andes. ▼

◁

The condor, King of the Andes, is threatened with extinction.

The high paramo

The paramo is a unique habitat of hardy grasses and small, low-growing shrubs found only in the high plains of the northern Andes, 3,000 metres or more above sea level. No trees grow in the dark soils of the paramo. The roots of paramo plants penetrate deeply into the soil. They have small, thick leaves that are sometimes hairy to conserve heat, and their flowers grow close to the ground. One native plant is known as the Rose of the Andes because of its large, beautiful red and yellow flowers. Wild lupins, orchids and other flowers also grow there, as do abundant numbers of lichens, mosses and ferns.

The paramo is home to many animals, including deer, rabbits and various rodents, many of which are hunted by the Andean fox, also known as the paramo wolf. The most famous bird of the paramo (though also one of the rarest) is the Andean condor, the King of the Andes, a mighty bird that soars effortlessly on its huge, outstretched wings. Other birds of the paramo include eagles, caracara falcons, and even some species of hummingbirds, such as the Estella hummingbird, which can be found at altitudes of up to 4,500 metres.

WILD POTATOES

The wild potato was discovered growing in the Andes Mountains by people living in what is now the country of Peru and was first grown as a crop about 4,500 years ago. Wild potatoes grow where the climate is too cold for other crops, such as wheat or corn. Andean farmers know of more than 200 different varieties of potatoes growing in the mountains.

The Rocky Mountains

The Rocky Mountains are like the backbone of North America, stretching more than 4,800 kilometres from Alaska in the north, through western Canada, and down the lower 48 states from Montana to New Mexico.

The Rockies form the Continental Divide, separating rivers flowing west to the Pacific Ocean from those flowing east to the Atlantic. Some of the greatest rivers in North America have their beginnings in the Rockies, including the Missouri, the Columbia and the Rio Grande. In some places, this mighty mountain range forms a barrier 600 kilometres wide. The highest peaks in the Rockies are in the southern part of the range, which runs from New Mexico to Wyoming. The action of **glaciers** long ago played a major role

Crossing the rugged Rocky Mountains was a challenge to early American pioneers.

in shaping the landscape of the Rocky Mountains. Early explorers gave the mountains their name because the landscape was so rugged.

Because the Rocky Mountains run for such a distance north to south, they also cross a number of climate zones, and

The grizzly bear has just one enemy in the mountains: humans.

a wide variety of plants and animals are found in the different habitats of the Rockies. In the United States, the Rockies separate the broad plains of the east from the deserts of the west.

Rocky Mountain plants

The plant life across most of the Rockies can be divided into five main vegetation zones. The first zone, which reaches up to about 1,500 metres, consists of grassy plains. From there up to about 2,100 metres, sage brush, junipers and pinyon pines grow. Higher still, up to around 2,700 metres, is the montane vegetation zone, dominated by pines, Douglas firs and aspens. Above this is the subalpine zone. This zone, which extends up to around 3,500 metres, supports spruce, lodgepole pines and aspens. The fifth zone is the alpine zone, which lies above the tree line. Meadows of alpine flowers and grasses grow there.

Rocky Mountain animals

The northern Rockies are home to the timber wolf and caribou, animals that are not found further south in the range. Rocky Mountain goats and bighorn sheep live above the tree line in many parts of the range. Bears – including black, brown and grizzly – prowl among the trees, along with deer, elk, mink, mountain lions, wolverines and other animals. Chipmunks, moose and coyotes can be found down in the sheltered, grassy valleys between the mountains. The cold streams fed by pure water from the glaciers are home to a variety of fish, such as the cutthroat trout.

The Alps

The Alps are the largest mountain system in Europe. They form a curving chain about 1,000 kilometres long across the south-central area of the continent. The Alps run from southern Germany and Austria, down through Switzerland and northern Italy, between Italy and France, just about to the Mediterranean Sea.

At their widest, across Switzerland and parts of Italy and Germany, the Alps are 256 kilometres across. The highest peak, Mont Blanc, lies between France, Italy and Switzerland and rises 4,763 metres into the air. The word Alps comes from a Latin word meaning high mountains, which is why high-altitude habitats around the world are referred to as alpine habitats.

Much of the spectacular ruggedness of the Alpine landscape is the result of the glaciers that carved their way through the area during the last **ice age**. These shifted countless tonnes of earth and rock, and formed valleys, hollows and waterfalls. As the glaciers retreated, they left behind huge fields of rocky debris called moraines.

Alpine climate

The Alps generally have a typical highland climate, meaning that the weather is cooler and wetter than in the surrounding landscape. As with all mountain areas, the climate changes as the altitude increases, with the highest parts of the range being the coldest. The peaks of the Alps are snow-covered all the year round.

Startled marmots let out a piercing whistle to warn others of danger.

The climate of the Alps also varies from place to place across the range. The southern Alps are in a region of hot, dry summers and mild winters, whereas the northern Alps are in the middle of an area of temperate climate. Here, summers are warm, winters are cold and it can rain at any time of the year.

Alpine life

The glacier-carved, U-shaped valleys running between the Alps are broad and grassy. Broad-leaved trees, such as oak and beech, grow up the lower slopes of the mountains and are succeeded by the hardier evergreen conifers, such as pine, spruce and fir, as the altitude increases and conditions grow colder. Above the tree line are the Alpine meadows, where flowers grow in a riot of colour every spring. Higher still, hardy plants such as mosses and lichen cling to the bare rocks. Nothing grows in the permanent ice and snow cover of the highest peaks.

Shaped by ice, the Matterhorn is one of the most striking mountains of the Alps.

Many different kinds of animals live in the forests and meadows of the Alps. Among them is the ibex, a type of wild goat found up to about 3,000 metres above sea level. The ibex has a strong, muscular neck to support the weight of its large horns and is a sure-footed climber, leaping with ease from rock to rock. The graceful chamois, which resembles an antelope, is also a type of goat that grazes in the Alpine meadows. The marmot, an animal that looks like a large hamster, lives above the tree line. When alarmed, marmots let out a shrill whistle to warn others nearby of danger. The danger could take the form of a golden eagle flying overhead. Marmots make up a large part of this magnificent bird's diet.

Bighorn sheep

The bighorn sheep of the Rocky Mountains are very well adapted for life in tough, high-altitude conditions. Their specialized hoofs are soft and flexible, giving them a sure-footed grip on cliff faces. They climb well and can make spectacular leaps that help them escape from most mountain **predators**. They have keen eyesight, a highly-developed sense of smell and sharp hearing, all of which warn the sheep far in advance of any approaching danger.

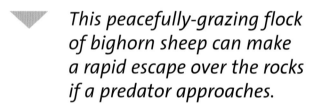

Winter coats

The bighorn sheep has a thick, beige coat of hair to keep out the winter cold. This double-layered, furry insulation is shed in the spring when the weather becomes warmer and then grows again as summer gives way to the chills of autumn.

This peacefully-grazing flock of bighorn sheep can make a rapid escape over the rocks if a predator approaches.

Big horns

Unlike deer and antelope, which shed their antlers every year, the bighorn sheep keeps its horns through its life. The size and shape of the horns show the age and sex of a particular sheep. The females' horns are straight and sharply pointed. They don't grow much after the sheep is four years old. By the time males are about eight years old, they have the big, curled horns that give the sheep their name. During the mating season, males make full use of their horns in head-clashing charges as they compete for females.

Like its horns, the bighorn's teeth also grow throughout its life. This is a good thing because the teeth are constantly being worn down by the sheep's diet of dry, gritty grass.

A bighorn sheep can live for up to 18 years, but most bighorns only live for about seven

It is easy to see how the bighorn sheep got its name.

WHAT A HEADACHE!

Charging male bighorns can collide with each other at speeds of more than 60 kilometres per hour. The noise made by their crashing horns can be heard 1.5 kilometres away!

or eight. Mountain life is tough in the winter, and many bighorns die as a result of the cold, lack of food, or an attack by hungry predators such as the mountain lion.

Mountain lions

The mountain lion, or puma, is among the top predators in the Americas. It can be found in an area that stretches from British Columbia, in Canada, south through Texas, Mexico, and Central America, then down to the tip of South America. The mountain lion is at home in the mountains, but it also lives in swamps, tropical forests and in near-desert conditions.

The mountain lion is a big cat with a fairly small head and short, rounded ears. Its upper body is covered with pale brown to tawny-coloured fur, and it has white and buff fur on its underbelly. It has a long, dark-tipped tail and long, heavy legs with large feet. A large male mountain lion can be 3 metres long from its nose to the tip of its tail, and weigh more than 90 kilograms.

Mountain hunter

The mountain lion is a solitary animal that hunts by day and by night, although when there are humans around it will keep well out of sight during the day. The mountain lion has a varied diet. It might prefer to hunt large animals such as deer, but it will not pass up a grasshopper or bird snack when it has the chance. It will also eat just about everything in between, including porcupines, beavers and coyotes.

◀ *The mountain winter is a tough time for all animals, including hunters such as the mountain lion.*

CALLS OF THE WILD

The mountain lion is usually a silent hunter, but it can produce a range of calls. It can give a piercing whistle when it has been cornered. Females in particular use this to warn their cubs. It also makes a terrifying call during the mating season that sounds like a person screaming in pain.

The mountain lion lies in wait to pounce on its **prey** or actively hunts it down, killing it with a powerful bite to the back of the neck. If the kill is too large to eat immediately, the mountain lion covers it with leaves, sticks and other materials and returns to it later.

The lion's life

Young mountain lions are usually born around midsummer every second year in a den lined with mosses or other plant material. On average, there are three cubs in a litter, weighing about half a kilo at birth. The cubs begin hunting with their mother at three months old. The youngsters take two years to develop enough skill to catch their own food reliably. Until then, they are taken care of by their mother. Barring accidents, a mountain lion will live between 10 and 20 years.

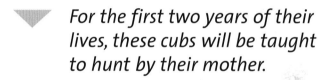

For the first two years of their lives, these cubs will be taught to hunt by their mother.

Golden eagles

The golden eagle is one of the most spectacular of mountain inhabitants. It is found across the world in North America, Europe, Asia and northern Africa. As well as patrolling the mountain areas, it also flies over canyons and grasslands in search of prey.

The golden eagle is a huge bird of prey with a wingspan of more than 2 metres. It soars effortlessly high in the sky, catching rising air currents with its broad wings. It is dark brown in colour, with a paler, golden-brown head. Its powerful, hooked beak is well suited to tearing the flesh of its prey, which it grips in the sharp, curved claws of its strong, yellow feet. Golden eagles have large eyes, and their eyesight is very sharp indeed, allowing them to spot their prey moving on the ground as they soar high above. Golden eagles can detect a rabbit moving more than 1.5 kilometres away.

The eagle's nest

Golden eagles build their nests, called eyries, on mountain ledges, craggy rock pinnacles, or in the branches of tall trees. Eyries are

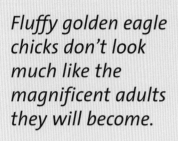

Fluffy golden eagle chicks don't look much like the magnificent adults they will become.

made of sticks and branches and are large and wide. Eagles will return to reuse the same eyries year after year, often adding to them each breeding season. An old nest can be up to 3 metres deep.

Every year, a female golden eagle lays two eggs and looks after them until they hatch around six weeks later. The male brings his mate food and occasionally takes a turn at **incubating** the eggs, too.

The newly-hatched eagles are covered in white **down** and scarcely resemble the powerful adults. The adults bring food to the nest until the chicks are old enough to begin hunting for themselves at around 11 weeks old. Usually, only one of the eagle

The golden eagle swoops down on powerful wings to grab its prey in its strong claws.

chicks survives to adulthood, with the strongest chick taking most of the food that the adults provide. After spending the autumn learning hunting skills with its parents, the young eagle will fly off to establish its own territory.

Eagle food

Golden eagles catch medium-sized animals such as grouse, rabbits and hares. They also prey upon other birds, rodents and sometimes snakes and fish. They don't always swoop down from high above to catch their prey. Sometimes they fly close to the ground, taking their prey by surprise with a swift attack.

If an eagle cannot catch anything itself, it will eat the remains of any dead animals it finds, including deer and sheep. This has often led to eagles being blamed for killing deer or sheep.

Wild yaks

High in the Himalayan mountains of Tibet, between 4,300 and 6,300 metres above sea level, as high as any plants can be found, is the rugged home of the wild yak.

This hardy relation of the cow has a thick, brownish-black, woolly coat that is very shaggy. The yak has a broad head with long, curved horns that may be more than a metre long on the males and about half that size on the females. The yak has short legs and broad hoofs with large **dewclaws** that help it grip the sometimes treacherous surfaces of its mountain habitat. A full-grown male yak may be 3 metres long, stand more than 2 metres tall at the shoulder, and weigh 800 kilograms or more.

The thick-coated yak provides nourishing milk for the peoples of the cold, snowy Himalayas.

The yak's life

The yak, with its thick coat, is so well adapted to the cold conditions of the high mountains that it becomes distressed by warm temperatures. It is perfectly at home in temperatures of -40° Celsius. Conditions in the yak's habitat are so harsh that very little grows there, and the herds have to travel great distances to find enough lichens, grasses and herbs to eat. Despite its bulky appearance, the yak is a sure-footed climber capable of travelling up and down the mountainside.

During the summer months of June and July, yak herds head down to the lower plains to take advantage of the mosses and swamp plants that grow there. This is the time when the calves are born. As the temperature continues to rise throughout August, the herds retreat into the hills once more, climbing right up into the snow to escape the summer heat. A yak herd can include up to 200 females and their young. The males are mostly solitary animals, though a few males may form small groups.

THE DOMESTIC LIFE

Although the wild yak is an increasingly endangered **species**, there are around 12 million **domestic** yaks in the world. For the people of Tibet in particular, the yak is an important animal. It provides meat and milk, it is used for transport, and it is even a source of energy, as its dung (droppings) is burned as fuel.

The wild yak has few enemies apart from human hunters and the rare Tibetan wolf, but it is a shy and distrustful animal. The herd will gallop off, their tails up, if they become alarmed. If danger appears, a yak may charge towards it but pull up short before reaching it.

Wild yaks are now quite rare, but millions of domesticated yaks are used by the people of the Himalayas.

Threats to the mountains

Mountain habitats may seem remote from human activities, but they are becoming increasingly vulnerable.

One of the biggest threats to the mountain environment comes from sheep and cattle farmers driving their animals up into the alpine meadows to feed. Overgrazing by livestock results in less food for the wild animals to eat and in the wearing away of the soil. Humans out for fun as well as food can also cause damage to the mountains by constructing ski lifts and resorts, and by using off-road vehicles and snowmobiles in high mountain areas.

Climate change

Many people believe that human activities are altering climates by causing the world to warm up. Burning **fossil fuels** release gases into the atmosphere that trap the sun's heat close to the Earth's surface. Mountain habitats and the plants and animals that live there are particularly vulnerable to this warming effect. Mountain icefields and glaciers are shrinking at an alarming rate all over the world. Glaciers in the Alps are only half as big as they were a century ago.

 Riding on snowmobiles can be fun, but it can also do great damage to a fragile mountain habitat.

If current trends continue, Glacier National Park in the Rocky Mountains will have to be renamed by the end of this century, as there won't be any glaciers left there.

Some scientists estimate that a rise in the world's temperature of three degrees or so will shift the mountain climate zones upwards by about 500 metres. Animals at the top of the mountain ranges won't have anywhere left to go. Some of the world's rarest wildlife is at severe risk. Animals that are well adapted to cold conditions, such as the Tibetan yak, will struggle to survive as

If the Earth's climate continues to warm up, the glaciers of Glacier National Park may vanish altogether.

their homes disappear. People living on and around the mountain areas will also be affected by these changes. Floodwaters from melting glaciers and the **permafrost** of the alpine tundra could wash away farmland or trigger **avalanches**.

Watching the mountains

Many scientists believe that what we see happening today in the mountains could happen tomorrow in the lowland areas. Every continent has mountains, and so every continent has guards to warn of the dangers of climate change. Protecting these spectacular habitats from damage will benefit everyone.

Glossary

adaptation A characteristic of a living thing that allows it to survive in its environment. For example, the thick, woolly coat of the yak protects it from the chill of the high mountains.

alpine Of the high mountain regions.

altitude Height above the ground or sea level.

amphibians Types of animals, such as frogs and toads, with soft, moist skin, that spend at least part of their lives in water.

Antarctic Circle An imaginary line around the south polar regions.

atmosphere The layer of gases that surrounds the Earth.

avalanches Huge, destructive falls of snow, ice and rocks down the sides of mountains.

biomes Large areas of the environment with distinctive climates and plant types. Examples include forests, mountains and deserts.

camouflage To make something difficult to see because it is the same colour or shape as the background.

climate The general weather conditions in a particular area.

conifers Evergreen trees. Conifers bear cones and often have needle-like leaves.

dewclaws The bones behind the foot, which look like a backward-pointing toe, in deer and other animals.

domestic To do with the home. A domestic animal is one that has been tamed by humans for work, food or companionship.

down Fluffy feathers that act as an insulating layer, trapping body heat.

equator An imaginary line that runs around the middle of the Earth, dividing it into the northern and southern hemispheres.

fossil fuels Fuels such as coal, crude oil and natural gas that are formed from the remains of plants and animals that lived millions of years ago.

glaciers Slow-moving rivers of ice that move down from the snowfields at the tops of mountains.

habitat The place where a living thing makes its home. The environment that it is adapted to survive in.

hibernation A means by which some animals survive long, cold winters. Their breathing and heart rate slows, their body temperature drops, and they fall into a sleep-like state that lasts until conditions improve.

ice age A period in Earth's history when the average temperature dropped and glaciers spread north and south from the polar regions. The last major ice age ended about 10,000 years ago.

incubating Sitting on eggs to keep them warm so they hatch.

migrate To move from one place to another in search of better living conditions.

nutrients Another word for food – all the things needed for a balanced diet which provides energy and raw materials for the growth and maintenance of an organism.

permafrost A layer of soil that is permanently frozen.

pollinators Animals such as insects, birds, and bats that carry pollen (small grains necessary for plant reproduction) from one flower to another.

predators Animals that catch and eat other animals for food.

prey Animals that are caught and eaten by predators.

radiation Energy that travels from one place to another as particles, such as those given off by radioactive materials, or waves, such as light and heat.

reptiles Cold-blooded animals, including snakes and lizards, with a dry, scaly skin. Most reptiles lay soft-shelled eggs and live on land.

species A group of living things with the same general appearance and behaviour, which can breed together to produce fertile offspring.

temperate zone The area between the tropics and the polar regions where the climate is moderate, without extremes of temperature or rainfall.

tundra The region of the cold north where there is a layer of permafrost beneath the topsoil, few trees can grow, and the vegetation is mainly grasses and mosses.

vegetation The plant life in an area.

Index